NOV - - 2016

How Many Minutes?

by Katherine Krieg

Say Hello to Amicus Readers.

You'll find our helpful dog, Amicus, chasing a ball—to let you know the reading level of a book.

1 Learn to Read

Frequent repetition, high frequency words, and close photo-text matches introduce familiar topics and provide ample support for brand new readers.

2 Read Independently

Some repetition is mixed with varied sentence structures and a select amount of new vocabulary words are introduced with text and photo support.

3 Read to Know More

Interesting facts and engaging art and photos give fluent readers fun books both for reading practice and to learn about new topics.

Amicus Readers are published by Amicus
P.O. Box 1329, Mankato, MN 56002
www.amicuspublishing.us

Photo Credits: Thinkstock, cover, 8; Shutterstock Images, 1, 4–5, 6, 14–15, 16 (top); Jen Siska/Thinkstock, 3; iStockphoto, 7; Antigoni Goni/Shutterstock Images, 11; Olga Popova/Thinkstock, 12, 16 (bottom)

Produced for Amicus by The Peterson Publishing Company and Red Line Editorial.

Editor Jenna Gleisner
Designer Becky Daum

Library of Congress
Cataloging-in-Publication Data
Krieg, Katherine, author.
  How many minutes? / by Katherine Krieg.
      pages cm. -- (Amicus readers. Level 2)
(Measuring time)
  Summary: "Introduces activities young readers experience in a matter of minutes, such as waiting in line at a carnival, while teaching ways to measure minutes and how they compare to seconds and hours."-- Provided by publisher.
  Audience: K to grade 3.
  ISBN 978-1-60753-721-2 (library binding)
  ISBN 978-1-60753-825-7 (ebook)
  1. Time--Juvenile literature. 2. Time measurements--Juvenile literature. I. Title.
  QB209.5.K75 2014
  529.7--dc23
                                    2014048038

Printed in Malaysia
10 9 8 7 6 5 4 3 2 1

We use minutes to measure time. There are 60 seconds in 1 minute. How many minutes can you spend at a carnival?

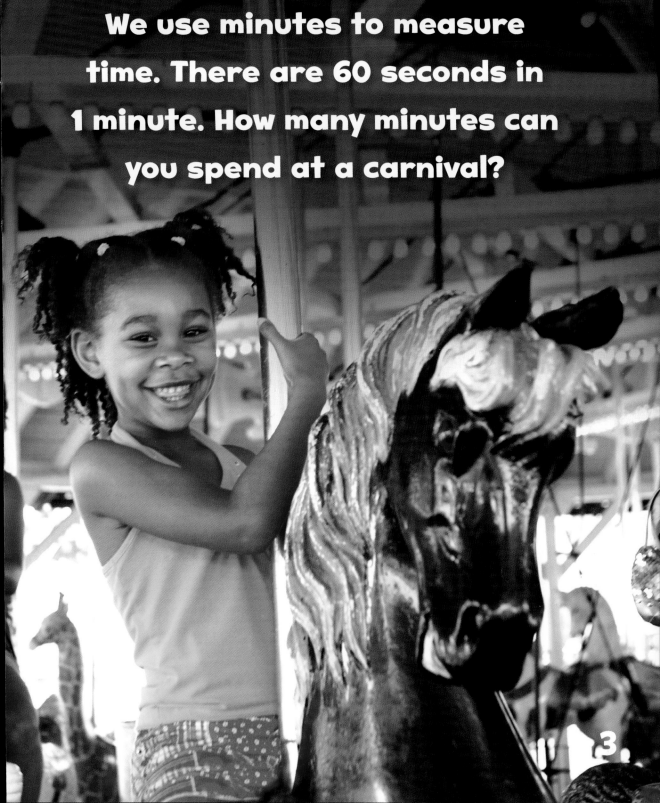

Cam throws 3 darts in
1 minute.

He tries to pop balloons.
One pops!

Luis times Mia eating cotton candy. He uses his digital watch. It takes her **3 minutes.**

Kevin waited to ride the roller coaster. He stood in line for **15 minutes** before riding.

Kate watches a clown show. The show lasts **30 minutes.** Thirty minutes is called a **half hour.**

minute hand

The minute hand on Grant's wristwatch has gone around 1 time. He has been at the carnival for

60 minutes.

That is the same as

1 hour.

There are lots of great things to do at the carnival that take a few minutes.

How many minutes would you like to stay?

Measuring Minutes

minute hand

hour hand

second hand

hours

minutes